DUDLEY SCHOOLS
LIBRARY SERVICE

KU-337-328

Schools Library and Information Services

S00000748056

Instruments and Music

Woodwind

Daniel Nunn

www.raintreepublishers.co.uk
Visit our website to find out more information about Raintree books.

To order:
☎ Phone 0845 6044371
▤ Fax +44 (0) 1865 312263
▧ Email myorders@raintreepublishers.co.uk

Customers from outside the UK please telephone +44 1865 312262

Raintree is an imprint of Capstone Global Library Limited, a company incorporated in England and Wales having its registered office at 7 Pilgrim Street, London, EC4V 6LB – Registered company number: 6695582

Text © Capstone Global Library Limited 2012
First published in hardback in 2012
The moral rights of the proprietor have been asserted.

All rights reserved. No part of this publication may be reproduced in any form or by any means (including photocopying or storing it in any medium by electronic means and whether or not transiently or incidentally to some other use of this publication) without the written permission of the copyright owner, except in accordance with the provisions of the Copyright, Designs and Patents Act 1988 or under the terms of a licence issued by the Copyright Licensing Agency, Saffron House, 6–10 Kirby Street, London EC1N 8TS (www.cla.co.uk). Applications for the copyright owner's written permission should be addressed to the publisher.

Edited by Dan Nunn, Rebecca Rissman, and Sian Smith
Designed by Joanna Hinton-Malivoire
Picture research by Mica Brancic
Production by Victoria Fitzgerald
Originated by Capstone Global Library Ltd
Printed and bound in China by Leo Paper Products Ltd

ISBN 978 1 406 22439 9 (hardback)
15 14 13 12 11
10 9 8 7 6 5 4 3 2 1

DUDLEY PUBLIC LIBRARIES

L

748056   Bel

J 788·05

British Library Cataloguing in Publication Data
Nunn, Daniel.
  Woodwind. -- (Instruments and music)
  1. Woodwind instruments--Juvenile literature.
  I. Title II. Series
  788.2'19-dc22

Acknowledgements
We would like to thank the following for permission to reproduce photographs: Alamy pp. 15 (© Lebrecht Music and Arts Photo Library/Chris Stock), 16 (© Sue Cunningham Photographic); © Capstone Publishers pp. 21 (Karon Dubke), 22 (Karon Dubke); Corbis pp. 13 (© Bob Krist), 20 (© Anders Ryman); Getty Images p. 23 bottom (Comstock Images); Photolibrary pp. 4 (Polka Dot Images), 7 (imagebroker.net/Wolfgang Diederich), 8 (Bluemoon Stock/Harvey Edwards), 9 (Photos India RF), 10 (John Warburton-Lee Photography/Christian Kober), 18 (Imagebroker.net/Heiner Heine), 19 (Image Source), 23 middle (Image Source); Shutterstock pp. 5 recorder (© Alexey Fursov), 5 flute (© Dragon_Fang), 5 ocarina (© Ilya Rabkin), 5 panpipes (© Jiri Hera), 5 clarinet (© Mikeledray), 5 bagpipe (© Slavoljub Pantelic), 6 (Chad McDermott), 11 (© Ken Inness), 12 (© Ben Smith), 14 (© Tepic), 17 (Igor Normann), 23 top (Jack.Qi).

Cover photograph of a flute player in traditional Peruvian dress, reproduced with permission of © Corbis (Bob Krist). Back cover photograph of a woman playing a flute reproduced with permission of Photolibrary (Bluemoon Stock/Harvey Edwards).

We would like to thank Jenny Johnson, Nancy Harris, Dee Reid, and Diana Bentley for their assistance in the preparation of this book.

Every effort has been made to contact copyright holders of material reproduced in this book. Any omissions will be rectified in subsequent printings if notice is given to the publisher.

Contents

Woodwind instruments

recorder

tambourine

People play many instruments to make music.

People blow woodwind instruments.
Not all woodwind instruments are
made of wood.

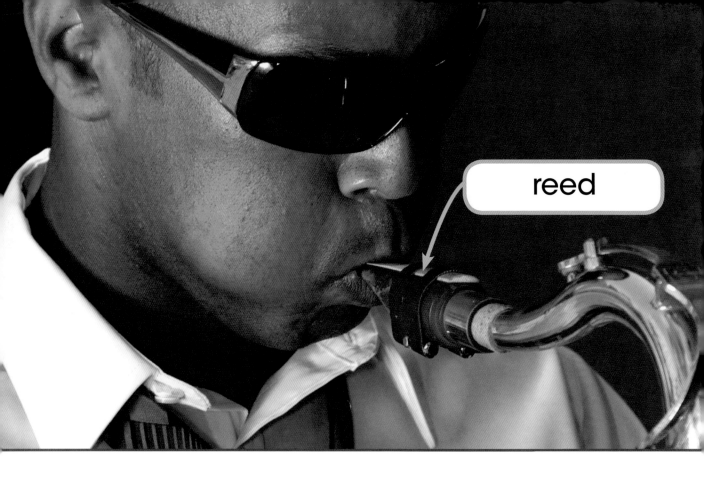

reed

People play by blowing on an edge
or a reed.

keys

People play notes by covering holes or pressing keys.

Flutes

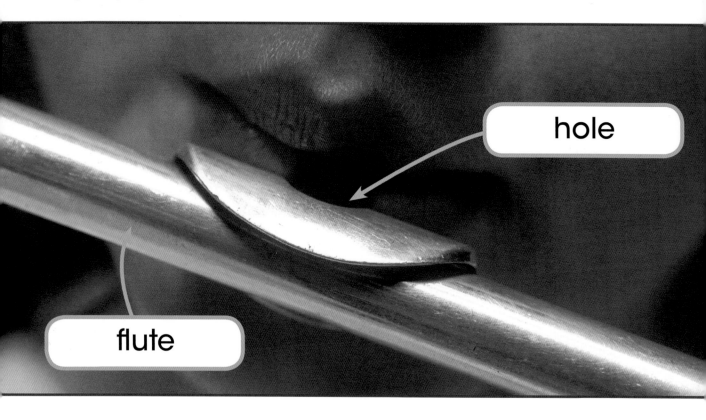

hole

flute

A flute makes a sound when people blow across the edge of a hole.

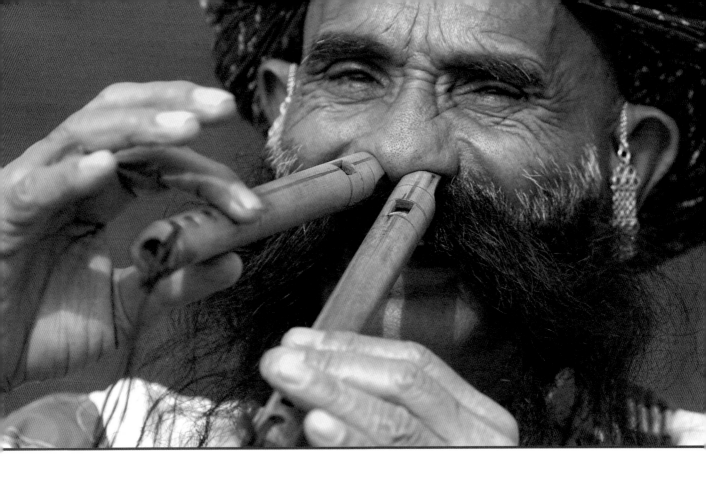

A nose flute makes a sound when
people blow with their nose!

A dizi is a bamboo flute.

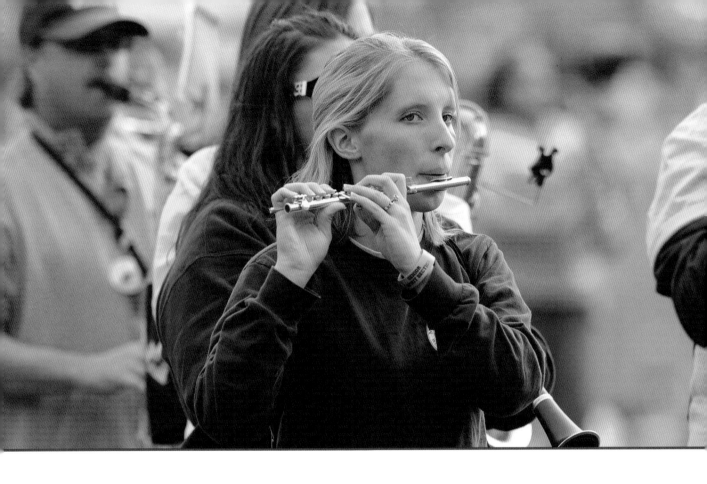

A piccolo is a small flute.

Reed instruments

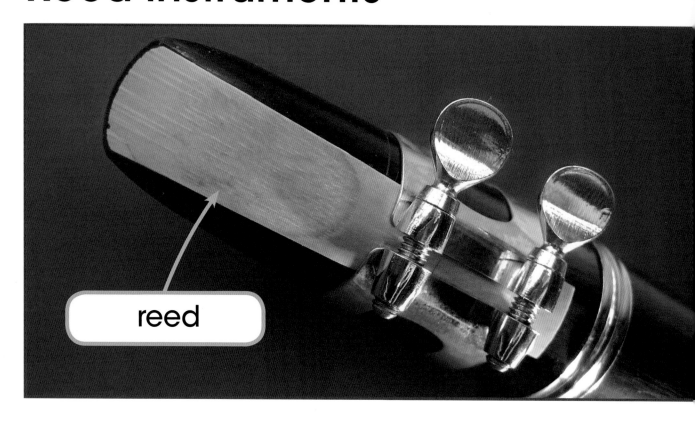

reed

A reed instrument makes sound when people blow against a reed.

The duduk is a very old reed instrument.

bag of air

Bagpipes make sound when you squeeze a bag full of air!

14

pipes

A mijwiz has two pipes instead
of one.

Playing woodwind instruments

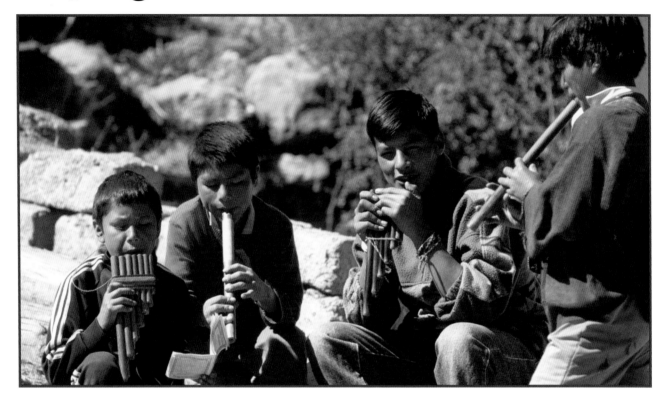

Some people play woodwind
instruments together.

saxophone

Some people play woodwind instruments on their own.

Some people play woodwind instruments for work.

Some people play woodwind
instruments just for fun!

Making woodwind instruments

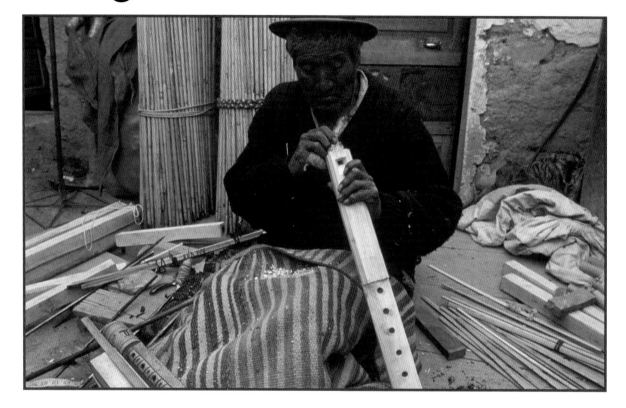

Some woodwind instruments are
hard to make.

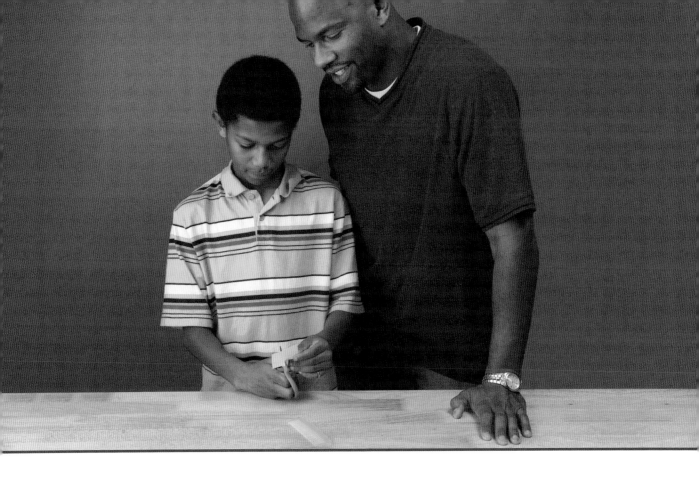

Some woodwind instruments are easy to make.

Play your own woodwind instrument

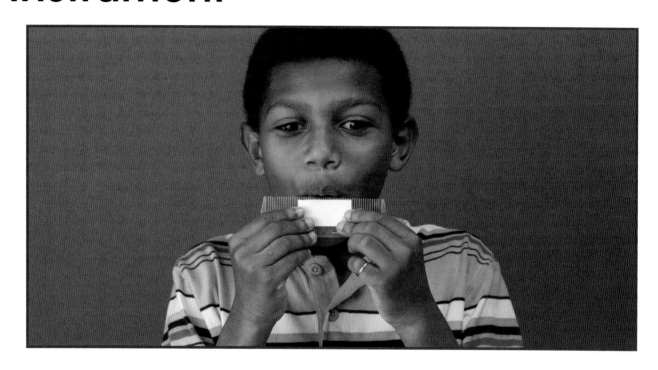

You can play your own woodwind instruments, too!

Picture glossary

 bamboo tall, woody grass with long, hollow stems

 note sound made by a musical instrument

 reed part of a woodwind instrument that moves when you blow on it to make a sound

Index

Notes for parents and teachers

Before reading

Show the children examples of woodwind instruments. Online examples with audio can be found at: http://ngfl.northumberland.gov.uk/music/orchestra/wind.htm Can they name any of the instruments? How do they think the instruments are played? Demonstrate if possible. Show the children a reed. Explain that an instrument is in the woodwind group when it is played by blowing air against a reed or against a sharp edge.

After reading

Encourage the children to make their own woodwind instrument. Get them to fill some old glass milk bottles with water and blow over the tops to make different sounds. The more liquid in the bottle, the higher the sound (because there is less air to vibrate).

Extra information

The instruments shown on page 5 clockwise from the top are: recorder, flute, clarinet, panpipes, ocarina, and bagpipes.
The different types of woodwind instruments are: flute-type instruments, where the player blows over an edge to make a sound (e.g. recorder); single-reed instruments (e.g. saxophone); double-reed instruments (e.g. oboe); and vibrating-reed-in-a-frame instruments (e.g. harmonica).